THE MERIT SYSTEM

Edwin Sánchez

I0139937

BROADWAY PLAY PUBLISHING INC
New York
www.broadwayplaypublishing.com
info@broadwayplaypublishing.com

THE MERIT SYSTEM
© Copyright 2016 by Edwin Sánchez

First printing: December 2016
I S B N: 978-0-88145-669-1

Book design: Marie Donovan
Typographic controls: Adobe InDesign
Typeface: Palatino

CHARACTERS

CUCA, 40, *recently divorced and entering the work force for the first time.*

RAYMOND, 32, *young executive on his way up.*

CAMMY, 35, CUCA's *co-worker, former sister-in-law and best friend.*

Various off stage voices will be heard through the play. Connie, RAYMOND's *fiancee, is a presence during many of his scenes.*

The action of the play takes place during the course of one year, 1977.

(Christmas tree lights are turning on and off on the left side of the stage. The lights are bright and colorful. For a moment these are the only lights we see. Lights up. The stage is divided in two. On the left is the living room of CUCA and Raul's Lower East Side apartment. Chair, sofa, stereo set and in the center of the living room, the blinking Christmas tree. CUCA is standing by the tree, staring transfixed at its colorful lights. She is an attractive woman of forty who is always "overdone". Her hair is bleached blonde, her makeup is gaudy, her clothing skin tight. She is carrying boxes to store the Christmas decorations. She puts the boxes down and continues to stare at the tree, lost in its gaudy beauty. This is not a particularly tasteful tree. It is a lot like CUCA.)

(Lights up on other side of the stage. A simple and tastefully decorated bedroom. Enter RAYMOND. He is a man of 32 wearing a trench coat and an expensive suit. In one hand he carries a leather briefcase and in the other a small paper bag. He turns on his T V and takes off his shirt and tie. Sitcom noise is barely audible in the background. He strips down to his socks and undershorts. He pulls out an old tee shirt from under his pillow and puts it on. He sits on the edge of the bed and pulls out some papers and a text book from his briefcase. He opens his text book and tries to study. He retrieves his paper bag and pulls a bottle of rum from it. He opens it and takes a drink directly from the bottle.)

RAYMOND: I can do this. I can do this. I can do this.

(CUCA yanks out the electrical cord from the wall and the tree goes dark. She gently removes some ornaments and carefully places them in a box. After she has filled the first

box, she places it on the floor behind the arm chair. On her way back she caresses the head rest. She turns on the radio and softly sings along with a ballad in Spanish. RAYMOND *is falling asleep in front of his T V. She stops singing. She returns to removing the tree decorations. After a few beats she pushes the tree to the ground and storms out. He tries to shake himself awake. He grabs his phone and dials.)*

RAYMOND: Hi, Connie. Can you come over. Just jump in a cab and come on over.

(Factory)

(A factory whistle is heard.)

*(*CAMMY, *has her arm around* CUCA.*)*

CUCA: I've never worked anywhere before. Never.

(Whenever CUCA *speaks to anyone it is understood that she is speaking Spanish. She doesn't speak English.)*

CAMMY: It's not like brain surgery, Cuca.

CUCA: I know. I know.

CAMMY: You talk to Raul?

*(*CUCA *shrugs in response.)*

CAMMY: You miss him?

CUCA: I miss parts of him.

CAMMY: Bet I know what part you miss most.

CUCA: If you do, tell me.

*(*CAMMY *addresses a group of factory workers.)*

CAMMY: Lissen, this is my friend, Cuca. Cuca she don't speak too good English, so if the foreman tells her to do something you explain it to her, okay? She never work before. Now she's a career girl, like us. What? Where? *(She looks at her skirt and sees a spot.)* So what? I'll buy a better one tomorrow. Maybe I'll buy two.

(CAMMY *pulls* CUCA *to a counter where they both pantomime doing piece meal work. They remain lit. Lights up on* RAYMOND *who is holding a report in his hands.)*

RAYMOND: I've read and reread the reports, sir, and I'm almost sure they're right, as far as I can tell. I may have made a mistake. Not intentionally, of course. You're right, relax. What's wrong? No, that's just a percentage. I thought that's what you wanted in that column. I must have misunderstood. I could have sworn you said percentage. No, of course, you're right. I'll redo it. I'm sorry. I'm sorry.

(Lights change.)

CAMMY: Never fall in love with an anal retentive. I'm telling you this as a friend. You don't win. You don't ever get to win. You gotta be wrong all the time.

CUCA: You don't have to tell me, I was married to one.

CAMMY: Hey watch what you say about my brother. Raul was not that bad.

CUCA: So, you're saying it was me? ...I wish I had been enough.

CAMMY: I saw him the other night. He cries a lot. Papi had to get him drunk to shut him up.

CUCA: What do you want me say?

CAMMY: Nothing. Lissen, you were unhappy, you left. End of soap opera.

CUCA: Yeah. ...He's probably the best man I'll ever have in my life.

CAMMY: You know it. But hey, at least you had one. Even if all you did was throw him away.

CUCA: I just think I deserve better. I've never had it, but I know I deserve it.

CAMMY: Better than him you ain't gonna get. Come on, let's go. *(She begins to put her coat on.)* The wind whips right through you. No respect for your bones.

(CAMMY and CUCA are about to exit. CUCA is looking around.)

CAMMY: It just looks glamorous, but it ain't.

(CAMMY exits. CUCA sees RAYMOND in a corner. He takes a small bottle from his pocket and quickly drinks from it. He shudders, puts the bottle away, takes a bite of some licorice and straightens his tie.)

RAYMOND: *(To himself)* Ready for you, Mr Stark. *(He exits.)*

(CAMMY reenters.)

CAMMY: Hey Cuca, the train don't stop here. We have to go to the station.

CUCA: Yeah, okay. …What kind of medical plan do you give here?

(Lights out on CAMMY and CUCA, up on RAYMOND's bedroom. He is on the phone, popping aspirin. Two at first, then another two. During the phone conversation he will close the aspirin bottle, open it and take another aspirin.)

RAYMOND: So, okay, I get there for the test and I can feel the veins on my temple throbbing as if they were outside my body. This, before I even sit down and get my number two pencil out. So, I'm sitting, I'm there like fifteen minutes before the test, I'm getting to that, and the teacher doesn't even acknowledge me and I don't know if I'm supposed to acknowledge him or not. I mean, he's the teacher, right? He does this everyday, this is the first written test I've taken in a hundred years. My head is pounding, and we sit there in silence. I'm about to take my text book out, one last brush up, and without looking up he says, "Please, put your books away." Like if he's talking to forty people.

Never looked up. So I spend ten minutes reading my number two pencil until...oh, I aced the test, I think, that's not the point. Okay...no, not a drop, I swear. Yeah. I love you, too. Say goodnight to baby Sigmond or Tallulah. Okay.

(RAYMOND *hangs up the phone. He opens a beer and a bag of chips, his dinner. He turns on the T V and sitcom music plays as he leans back.)*

(CUCA's apartment. CAMMY and CUCA are watching a telenovela.

CAMMY: *(To the T V character)* Hit him! Hit him! Look at her, she lowers her head and bats her eyelashes. Asshole. I swear a man touch me, I'll cut his hand off.

CUCA: My first husband beat me.

CAMMY: I hope you hit him back.

CUCA: He'd a killed me.

CAMMY: Always push a bully back.

CUCA: I was a brunette then.

CAMMY: Hit him back, and if he's too big, hit him with a two by four.

CUCA: He'd leave in one mood and come back in another. You just could never tell.

CAMMY: *(Referring to the T V character)* Look at the little band aid they put on her. He pimped slapped her and she shows up with a little band aid over her eye.

CUCA: The first smack would come out of nowhere, always when I was looking away from him. I would try not to look at him because my eyes would make him crazy.

CAMMY: *(Referring to the T V character)* She is so beautiful.

CUCA: The man was born angry. *(Referring to the T V)* Yeah, now they kiss.

CAMMY: And yes, yes yes, we're getting some tongue action!!!

CUCA: Beer?

CAMMY: I'll force myself.

(CUCA exits, reenters with two beers.)

CAMMY: So, how did you become a liberated woman and leave that house of abuse?

CUCA: I didn't leave, he kicked me out. Used to say he would kill me if I left him, but then he found somebody else. Brought her home. She has my bed, all the furniture I picked out, my first washing machine.

CAMMY: Yeah, but she also got him, so don't get too gooey eyed. He probably keeps her stuck to his fist.

CUCA: No, she looks great. He looks like he's aged fifty years.

CAMMY: *(Referring to the T V character)* I hate that bitch. What the hell does he see in her? She's so ugly.

CUCA: She owns everything.

CAMMY: That's the only way she can get a man into her bed.

CUCA: And she just keeps getting married.

CAMMY: Look who's talking.

CUCA: Three is not the same as eight.

CAMMY: If you say so. Look how he's touching her. Now, that man has finesse. Softly. Softly. No rush. She can barely feel his touch. Oh, if I were an actress I'd be in rehearsal twenty four hours a day.

(CAMMY and CUCA watch in silence.)

CAMMY: Go baby!!! The shirt's coming off! Yes! The shirt… The shirt is history!!

CUCA: They're married to other people.

CAMMY: But they look so good together.

CUCA: You said she was ugly.

CAMMY: Well, he makes her look good. Beauty by osmosis. What I wouldn't give to be a bead of his sweat. Travel that road.

(CAMMY *and* CUCA *watch in silence.*)

CUCA: My second husband cheated on me.

CAMMY: It's a bitch watching a soap with you, you know that?

(CUCA *laughs.*)

CUCA: They're amateurs.

CAMMY: I guess so. (*Referring to the T V*) Oh, why are they cutting to them? I don't care about those people. (*To* CUCA) See, that's in you, forgive my frankness. Right from the beginning you set up the rules. No hitting, no cheating.

CUCA: How many times you been married?

CAMMY: None.

CUCA: Then shut up. You talk more than you watch the damn show.

CAMMY: You're the one trying to top the divas, don't take it out on me.

(CAMMY *and* CUCA *watch in silence.*)

CAMMY: I know Raul had his faults, but my brother never hit you, and to my knowledge he never put the horns on you, so why? If you were waiting for a good man, he was it.

CUCA: He should have been.

(RAYMOND *and his fiancee, Connie are browsing in a furniture store. We never see Connie.*)

RAYMOND: *(To salesperson)* We're just looking, thank you. *(To Connie)* Connie, we can't afford this stuff. I know that our salaries combined could do this but what if I lose my job? You don't know. We start getting into all kinds of debt until all of a sudden at work they discover there's not there there when it comes to me. Yes, the sectional is very nice. *(Loudly)* I just got the damn promotion. *(Lowering his voice)* I don't care how many people do it. I would like to wait a bit before I get into hock for all of eternity. I'm sorry. Let's not fight. Lead the way. I'll leave the baby room totally up to you. *(She is busy checking out some furniture. He talks to her back.)* I'm drowning here, do you understand? I've got a great boss who's given me a promotion no one else thinks I deserve and a beautiful woman who overloves me. And you're going to give me another son, right? This will replace the son I never see. God, I'm lucky. I'm drowning in luck. My father was a janitor and I wear a tie to work. Can you explain that to me, Connie? Can you?

(Lights out on RAYMOND. *Up on* CUCA. *She arrives home, exhausted. She takes off her shoes, puts a tape on the cassette player and puts on head phones. She flops into a chair. As the music play she begins to softly cry. She folds over and as she does the headphones come off and we faintly hear a bolero. Lights out.)*

(Lights up. RAYMOND *at bar, during happy hour.)*

RAYMOND: Couldn't be better. Connie and I are back on track. Ah, well we have a fight every week. No big deal. Baby Heathcliff or Samantha is on the way and I'm the boss's fair haired boy. Man. It's a figure of speech, asshole. No, I got the next round. Oh come on, it's early. I don't want to go just yet. I'm supposed to meet Connie at her parents. A lovely weekend with the Moores, and without the firm foundation of a drink it just ain't gonna happen. Two days where the smell of alcohol is but a memory. *(He downs his drink.)* Get it while you can.

(Lights out. Up on CUCA, *riding the subway. She is half asleep. Even though it is very early she is fully made up for work in her usual gaudy fashion. A garbled message is heard over the train loud speaker. She can't understand it.)*

CUCA: What he say? What he say?

MAN'S VOICE: What's the matter, lady? Don't you speak English?

CUCA: He talk too fast. *(She gets off the train, her destination is her usual cafeteria.)*

COOK: *(V O)* Watch this. Everyday she comes in and asks for the same thing. "Ham and eggs". I bet she can't say anything else.

*(*CUCA *looks around at what would be the counter. Her eyes stop at a plate and she smiles broadly.)*

CUCA: Taste.

COOK: *(V O)* Taste? Taste what? Whaddya wanna taste?

CUCA: *(Less sure of herself)* Taste.

COOK: *(V O)* Look, I ain't got all day. What is this taste business?

CUCA: *(Exasperated)* Ham and eggs.

(Lights up on factory. A whistle blows. CAMMY *practically leaps up.)*

CAMMY: Pee break! They clock you so you gotta pee fast.

(In the background, RAYMOND *enters, he is holding a folder. He rips it in half and throws it away. He exits.* CUCA *picks*

up one of the torn sheets from the report that was in the folder. She looks at it, shrugs and throws it away.)

CAMMY: Hey, you're purse. Hello?

(CUCA grabs her purse.)

CUCA: I'm sorry. My mind is someplace else today.

CAMMY: You mean it's not here? In this little slice of heaven.

CUCA: *(Laughs)* Fool.

CAMMY: You doing overtime tonight?

(CUCA nods.)

CAMMY: Now who's the fool?

CUCA: I need the money, honey. I gotta move.

CAMMY: Why? Raul left you the apartment, which no offense I would not have done. Sorry.

CUCA: I don't mean apartments. I gotta go someplace else. It's like he's still there. I see him everywhere. I'm not gonna be able to fix my heart there.

CAMMY: You just want permission to be selfish. Don't dress it up, that's all it is.

(RAYMOND is sitting at his desk at his night class.)

RAYMOND: *(Turning to someone on his left)* I know I had it with me when I left. I mean, I did the assignment, I'm not trying to get away with anything here. This is not like me, I don't lose things. I'm not dumb, you know. I just got a mind like a sieve. I can't retain anything. My boss wants to see what grade I get in this course. I'm trying. I swear to God I'm trying.

(Lights out on RAYMOND, up on CAMMY and CUCA.)

CAMMY: *(Laughing)* Dummy, it's toast! So you're standing there screaming, "Taste, Taste!" Poor thing. You got your thermos?

CUCA: Yes.

CAMMY: When you get out it's gonna be late. Remember, carry your money in your inside pocket, like this, and always keep a token in your hand.

CUCA: Yes, grandma.

CAMMY: Don't stay too late. Don't have to make these bastards richer than they already are. You know what I mean.

CUCA: Yes, yes.

CAMMY: And take a break for dinner. I'll see you tomorrow.

(CAMMY and CUCA kiss each other on the cheek. RAYMOND is in his office on the phone.)

RAYMOND: Voice mail, thank God, okay. Look, Connie sweetheart, I'm not gonna be able to make it tonight. Class was not too productive so I'm back at work to earn some brownie points. Talk to you tomorrow? I'm sorry. *(He hangs up. He takes a small bottle of liquor from his briefcase and drinks from it.)*

(CUCA gets up from her work station and stretches. She takes out a compact from her purse and checks her face. She takes her bag. RAYMOND takes his briefcase and a brown paper bag. They are both heading to the executive dining room.)

RAYMOND: Excuse me, this is off limits for factory personnel.

CUCA: I no speak English. No English.

RAYMOND: Well, English is all you're going to get from me. *(He points for her to leave.)* You don't belong here. *(He points to himself.)* Executive.

CUCA: I'm telling you I don't understand. I know very little English and when I'm nervous I forget the little I do know.

RAYMOND: Hey, watch that. I can't believe you people come here and don't know the language. I mean that's just plain stupid. You don't understand a word I'm saying, do you?

CUCA: Same to you.

RAYMOND: You can't eat here. This room is for very important people. You no eat here.

(RAYMOND *stresses each of these words as if to help* CUCA *understand. She points to his paper bag.*)

RAYMOND: That's different. I'm a very important person.

CUCA: You're not prettier than I am.

(RAYMOND *enters the dining area and prepares to eat his take out Chinese.* CUCA *enters.*)

RAYMOND: Hey lady, I said no. Are you deaf as well as stupid.

(CUCA *sits and unwraps her sandwich, which she made at home.* RAYMOND *goes up to her but is seduced by the smell of her meal.*)

RAYMOND: What is that?

CUCA: No go.

RAYMOND: *(Pointing to her sandwich)* That. What's that?

CUCA: Pernil.

RAYMOND: Look, I don't want to have to fire you because that's not my style but I'm going to have to write you up a memo.

(CUCA *offers* RAYMOND *some of her sandwich.*)

RAYMOND: Okay, you can stay. But just this time. That's all I need, for my boss to catch me eating with you. No, I don't want any of your sandwich. This is what you're supposed to eat when you work late. You order Chinese. All the executives do. You don't bring food from home.

(CUCA *takes some "Ding Dong" cupcakes from her bag.*)

RAYMOND: I don't believe you. You probably have some Hawaiian Punch in there too.

CUCA: At least I offered.

RAYMOND: Speak English.

(CUCA *takes out her thermos and pours herself some coffee.*)

CUCA: Café?

RAYMOND: Okay, that I will have.

(RAYMOND *approaches* CUCA *with a cup and she pours him some.*)

CUCA: Hot.

(RAYMOND *takes a sip.*)

RAYMOND: It's hot, but it's good. Let me cool it down a bit. *(He takes some liquor from his briefcase and pours some into his cup.)* Medicine.

(CUCA *shrugs as if to say, "It's no concern of mine".*)

RAYMOND: You speak a little English, don't you?

CUCA: *(Offering him a cupcake)* Ding dong?

RAYMOND: I can see you're covering the four basic food groups. You know you're going to kill yourself with that diet of yours. *(He picks up a Ding Dong and shakes his head emphatically.)* No good.

CUCA takes the other Ding Dong and pops the whole thing in her mouth.

CUCA: Mmm good.

RAYMOND: Cute. But you can't get by on cute forever. Someday you'll have to be a person of substance. I mean, look at you, you look like a clown with that make up. No offense.

(RAYMOND *points to* CUCA*'s face, she smacks his hand
away.*)

RAYMOND: Hey, excuse me for giving you some
friendly and highly needed advice.

(CUCA *takes out her compact and looks at her face. She takes
a cigarette from her bag, lights it and takes only two puffs
before putting it out.*)

RAYMOND: What the hell was that about?

CUCA: *(Pointing to cigarette)* Bad. Very bad.

RAYMOND: Right. Have another Ding Dong. *(He pours
some more liquor into his cup and drains it.)*

CUCA: That's not so good. You don't care a thing about
yourself, do you?

RAYMOND: Be careful, you never know what I'll
understand. *(Offering her some of his food.)* You want
some of this? I'm not really that hungry.

(CUCA *shakes her head "no".*)

RAYMOND: Yes ma'am. I eat right, I talk right, I dress
right. I should be able to fit in with no problem. Hey
lady, this ain't getting any easier. What am I doing
wrong?

(CUCA *begins to pack her belongings away.*)

RAYMOND: It's probably not a good idea for you to eat
here, but there's hardly anybody here at this hour. So,
I guess if you're doing overtime again, it's okay. Here
I am, wasting my breath and you probably don't even
understand me.

CUCA: Bye bye.

RAYMOND: Yeah, you too, lady.

CUCA: *(Points to herself)* Cuca.

(CUCA gives RAYMOND a Ding Dong and exits. After she is leaves he pops the whole thing in his mouth and eats it. Lights out)

(Lights up on a subway platform. RAYMOND enters, he slows down when he notices CUCA, who is also waiting.)

RAYMOND: I would have walked you here if I'd known you were taking the same train.

CUCA: It's okay.

RAYMOND: Kind of late for a woman to be riding the subway alone. Let me give you a piece of advice. Never ride in the first or the last car, that's where all the punks hang out.

CUCA: It's okay.

(CUCA pulls out a rat tail comb from her pocket. RAYMOND snorts to himself.)

RAYMOND: How long have you been waiting? *(He points to his watch.)* Time, how much you wait? *(He is exasperated by her inability to answer him. He looks past her down the darkened tunnel. He pulls out a copy of Crain's Business Week and begins to read.)*

CUCA: Fifteen minutes.

(RAYMOND ignores CUCA. The train arrives. They board it. She waits until he sits then sits next to him.)

CUCA: Safer.

(RAYMOND looks up, sees the man in front of CUCA.)

RAYMOND: It's all right. He's just drunk. Probably doesn't even know we're on the same train.

CUCA: Go far?

RAYMOND: Me? Yeah, a rental in Jersey City.

(RAYMOND tries to go back to his paper. CUCA clears her throat.)

RAYMOND: Oh, and you?

(CUCA *beams. This is information she has memorized verbatim and repeats almost robot-like.*)

CUCA: Take the 2 train to Times Square where you will get off and go down a flight of stairs to the 7 train. Please take the 7 train to Queens Boulevard.

RAYMOND: See, you can learn when you want to learn.

CUCA: *(In English)* Why you work late? You boss.

(RAYMOND *puts his paper down and looks at* CUCA.)

CUCA: Sorry, you read.

RAYMOND: It's okay. I can't fit anything else into my brain tonight. I work late to catch up. Everybody thinks it's for brownie points, but I just want to catch up.

CUCA: You boss.

RAYMOND: I am *a* manager.

CUCA: You boss.

RAYMOND: *(Pointing to the drunk)* Actually, he's the boss. I wonder what he's drinking.

(CUCA *shrugs.*)

RAYMOND: So, you married? *(He pantomimes ring on finger.)*

CUCA: No more. *(She pantomimes taking ring off and throwing it away.)*

RAYMOND: Too bad, I guess. I'm getting married soon. *(He pantomimes putting a ring on.)*

CUCA: Oh yeah? First?

RAYMOND: Of course it's my first.

CUCA: Good. Don't forget her.

(CUCA *shows* RAYMOND *a drawing.*)

RAYMOND: What's this? Did you draw this?

CUCA: Me and house I buy in Puerto Rico.

RAYMOND: Cuca, don't tell me you're one of those who think that someday they will return to the island. Doesn't happen. Learn to love New York. You'll be here for a long time.

CUCA: My stop. *(Referring to her dream house.)* I do this.

RAYMOND: That's what they all say.

CUCA: All is not Cuca. *(She exits.)*

RAYMOND: Wanna bet?

(Lights change. CAMMY *and* CUCA.*)*

CAMMY: So what you gonna do with all the money you make from overtime?

CUCA: Save it.

CAMMY: For what? A down payment on a man?

CUCA: I had a man. A very good man.

CAMMY: The man was a saint.

CUCA: Is. He's not dead.

CAMMY: He might as well be dead as far as your concerned.

CUCA: Hey, you're the one who called me. "I can get you a job. No problem." Don't keep throwing him in my face.

CAMMY: Okay, okay. Holy virgin. It's like I wound you up. ...So, why did you leave? Don't tell me what you said in court. Why did you really, really leave?

CUCA: Because I didn't love him. In the beginning I did. I don't know when it changed. He never stopped loving me, or so he said. He wants to move to California. He wants me to go with him.

CAMMY: You don't love him, just a little?

CUCA: I tried to leave him for so long cause I knew I shouldn't be with him if I didn't love him. I even told him I didn't love him and he said, "that's okay".

CAMMY: I hate when they do that.

CUCA: Is he angry that I work with you?

CAMMY: He spit at me and called me a whore, but he took it well.

CUCA: I live with the image of him eating alone for the rest of his life. It breaks my heart.

CAMMY: Do you see yourself eating alone for the rest of your life?

CUCA: I just…I have a heavy heart. Lissen, do you want to have Chinese tonight?

CAMMY: Cuca, it's eight a.m., how can you be thinking about dinner?

CUCA: I'm abnormal.

(RAYMOND *is buttoning his shirt, looking at a row of ties.*)

RAYMOND: I saw my boss spill something on his tie and he just took it off and threw it away. I saw him later that same day and he was wearing another tie. It's like he keeps a fresh supply of them in his desk. Meanwhile I'm wearing his hand me down custom made suits with ties I buy from street peddlers. (*He pulls out a box of shoes from his closet and studies them for a moment.*) Ah no, oxblood. Go with the oxblood. (*He rushes into his suit.*) Sweetheart, you know I have a set routine in the morning. Trying to think of what I'm going to do and say for the rest of the day. I can't get into small talk.

CAMMY: So you're telling me you were late for work because you went for a ride?

CUCA: I got up late and by the time I got to the subway you were gone. And when the train comes I get on and fall asleep. I missed my stop. When I woke up I saw trees and houses outside. I thought to myself, "I'm already late", so I just stayed and watched. I never saw this side of New York. It was pretty, you know.

RAYMOND: The tie doesn't match. What is it? All of a sudden I'm not speaking English? The tie does not match. Yes, they will notice. Every mistake I make they notice.

CUCA: I figure I was already late, let me see how the other half lives. I want a house like the ones I saw.

CAMMY: Yeah, like you'll ever get it.

CUCA: I waited until the ride was over and then I came back. *(She lowers her head and cries.)*

RAYMOND: I feel like I'm putting on a disguise. I'm trying to pass and somebody's going to catch me. They're waiting for me to fall.

CAMMY: Sometimes I don't understand you.

(CUCA and RAYMOND at work. He sits in front of his desk going through some papers in his "In" box. He scans them, making notations on some, others he tosses out.)

(CUCA is repeating the same task over and over. She is using a small soldering iron on some tools. After she has done one dozen she packs up a small tray and piles her finished product on it. She has done two trays to which she adds a third.)

CUCA: Pick up.

(RAYMOND begins to high light passages in a memo he is reading. His phone buzzes.)

RAYMOND: Yes sir. Oh good, you got my report. No, I didn't mind doing it over again. I just want to do it right. I'm very glad you appreciate my work.

(CUCA's boredom increases. She begins to embellish her routine with some fancy touches. She burns herself slightly.)

CUCA: Carajo. *(She looks around to see if someone has heard her.)* Excuse me. *(She piles on the fourth tray.)* Hey, pick up! Pick up

RAYMOND: Yes sir. I can have that updated profit loss report to you in about an hour. No problem. Yes, I have decided what I want on my business card. "Raymond Rivers, Manager of Administration". ...Why, do you think I should use "Ray"?

CUCA: Cammy!

(CAMMY enters wearing a smock.)

CAMMY: So what is it?

CUCA: Where's the guy who's supposed to pick up my product?

CAMMY: *(Stomping her foot)* Hey! Pick up! Pick up!

RAYMOND: No, I think I'd rather have "Rivers". Easier to pronounce. Easier to remember. And don't worry about those figures, I have them right here in front of me. *(He reaches into his "In" box and can't find them. He plunges into his "Out" box, again not finding them.)* I'll be right up with them. *(He hangs up and searches desperately through his desk.)* I had them. I know I had them. *(He searches through his garbage.)*

(CAMMY and CUCA by the pay phones.)

CAMMY: *(Into receiver, very sensually)* Okay baby. I see you later. Yeah, wait for me at the subway station. I love you too.

CUCA: Liar, liar, pants on fire.

CAMMY: You know, maybe we can join a gym. I see they got a two for one membership, you know, you bring your best friend. You wouldn't mind going with me, would you? A great way to meet men.

CUCA: *(Referring to her phone call.)* What about Mister Right?

CAMMY: You mean Mister Right Now? He'll be a memory by payday. ...I admire what you did. No, seriously. Okay, it was my brother and all, but still, you were the one who left. I've never been able to do that. I always wanted to be the one who ended it. Be the dumper, not the dumpee. Not wear the dark glasses in the all night diner as I get the old heave ho at four a.m.. Burning my fingers because I can't keep my hand from shaking as I light his cigarette. And you know, they all hate to see you cry. They get pissed off. Like you're drawing attention to the fact that they're bastards.

CUCA: I haven't been dancing in so long.

CAMMY: What did I just say?

CUCA: Something about a gym.

CAMMY: I hate you.

CUCA: You can't live without me.

CAMMY: Same thing. So, what you are you gonna do this weekend?

CUCA: This weekend?

CAMMY: Let's go out. I'll take you to some crazy places.

CUCA: Clean the house. Go to the movies.

CAMMY: Lissen, don't you get a little horny every now and then?

CUCA: That's none of your business.

CAMMY: Not that there's anything wrong with sleeping alone. I can fart to my heart's content.

CUCA: Honey, I've been with you on the subway. You do it anywhere.

CAMMY: *(Laughs)* You're not supposed to notice.

CUCA: Yeah, and then you look around as if saying, "Who was the pig?"

CAMMY: You know me too well.

(RAYMOND *is in the executive dining room.* CUCA *enters.*)

RAYMOND: Hi, I had just about given up on you.

(CUCA *nods.*)

RAYMOND: Come on, you know how to say "hello", don't you?

CUCA: You make me nervous.

RAYMOND: *(Laughs)* You're lucky to be as ignorant as you are.

CUCA: Café?

(CUCA *pours* RAYMOND *half a cup.*)

RAYMOND: A little stingy on the coffee tonight.

CUCA: *(Referring to his liquor)* Your medicine.

RAYMOND: *(Pointing to her bag)* Oh right. Well, what gastronomic weapon are you going to commit suicide with tonight?

CUCA: Rice and beans. *(She points to his bag.)*

RAYMOND: Turkey on whole wheat. Hold the mayo.

CUCA: Turkey

(RAYMOND *points to his sandwich.*)

RAYMOND: Good. Turkey.

CUCA: Turkey.

(RAYMOND *points to himself.*)

RAYMOND: Turkey.

CUCA: Turkey.

(RAYMOND *pours some more liquor into his cup.*)

RAYMOND: Always, always, always, if you're going to drink at work make it Anisette. Then you keep a jar of licorice on your desk and tell anybody who asks that you're trying to quit somking. They'll think what they smell on your breath is licorice. Of course you've go to make sure not to weave and bob in the corridor. Want a taste?

(RAYMOND *offers* CUCA *some of his coffee. She refuses.*)

RAYMOND: Hey Cuca.

CUCA: Hey Turkey.

RAYMOND: Mister Turkey to you. Do you want me to read you the Turkey's letter or resignation? You understand of course that this is just a first draft and it will have to be corrected and recorrected by the powers that be. Hell, you don't understand any of this, do you? "Dear Mr Stark, due to circumstances beyond my control I must herein offer my resignation effective immediately. I feel I am unable to perform my duties to your exacting." Do you like exacting?

(CUCA *is eating her meal. She shrugs.*)

RAYMOND: Right. "Due to your highest standards. Please be aware that I in no way wish for you to compromise these standards. I should and must perform to your complete satisfaction and I feel…I feel…I feel I am a total fuck up."

(CUCA *laughs at this last phrase.*)

RAYMOND: Oh sure. That one you know. The man is good to me, Cuca. He's not just a boss, he's a generous friend. Well, no, he's an acquaintance. A friend is someone that if you fart in front of them they don't have a heart attack. What am I saying? Swear to me you don't speak English.

(CUCA *takes a candy bar out of her bag.*)

CUCA: Baby Ruth.

RAYMOND: Cuca, don't ever change. Coffee, please.

(CUCA *pours* RAYMOND *some and he doctors it.*)

RAYMOND: I never used to drink until I got this promotion. You know what I started out as? Mail room boy. And they gave me a test to make sure I knew how to read English. Now, I'm the only minority on the block. Oh, yeah. Allow me to introduce myself, Ramon Rivera alias El Kid alias Raymond Rivers. Don't know a word of Spanish, don't care to learn. So sorry we can't break into something a little reminiscent of the island. My island is Manhattan.

CUCA: Ramon Rivera is no turkey.

(RAYMOND *folds up his letter of resignation.*)

RAYMOND: I write about two of those a week. Some days are worse than others.

CUCA: Your name is Ramon Rivera.

RAYMOND: No, it used to be. Could you forget I told you that, please?

CUCA: If you Ramon Rivera you have to speak little bit of Spanish.

RAYMOND: Will you quit calling me that.

CUCA: Poor thing.

(CUCA *tries to smooth* RAYMOND's *brow, he jumps up.*)

RAYMOND: Hey watch it, lady. Keep your hands to yourself.

CUCA: *(Insulted)* Same to you. *(She angrily packs up her things.)*

RAYMOND: I apologize. I'm sorry. Stay. Please stay.

(RAYMOND *gently takes* CUCA's *bag, she thinks about it for a moment and decides to stay.*)

CUCA: Don't do that no more.

RAYMOND: Yeah, yeah, okay. I can't believe I told you. *(Blurts out)* I got a kid in Puerto Rico, you know. No, of course you don't know. A son. I was sixteen when he was born.

CUCA: Back to work. (*She rises to leave.*)

RAYMOND: My boy speaks Spanish. He lives on the island with his mother and her husband who he calls, "papi". Hey Cuca.

CUCA: What?

RAYMOND: My girlfriend is white. We're going to be married soon. I just thought you should know. I always wanted to be Archie Andrews when I was growing up. Forget it. Sometimes I'm totally surprised by what comes out of my mouth. You got any more coffee?

CUCA: No.

(CUCA *exits. After a couple of beats* RAYMOND *grabs the phone.*)

RAYMOND: Oh shit. Hello, are you there? I'm sorry I forgot to pick you up. Yes, we were supposed to do baby names tonight. Please let me make it up to you. I'm sorry.

(CAMMY *and* CUCA *exit the subway station.*)

CUCA: Damn, it's cold! I could be in Puerto Rico right now.

CAMMY: It's not that cold.

CUCA: I'm gonna open a savings account tomorrow.

CAMMY: You know what we should do? Get ourselves a bachelorette apartment and become roommates.

CUCA: No, I work hard for one year and have enough for a down payment on a house in Aibonito.

CAMMY: That's what you want, huh?

CUCA: I think so.

CAMMY: What else?

CUCA: I'd like to take a trip on a boat someday.

CAMMY: You never told me that.

CUCA: It doesn't have to happen tomorrow, as long as it happens.... I could win the lottery. I once asked Raul about his dreams and then I waited for him to ask me about mine. He laughed and told me, "Cuca, I know all your dreams."

CAMMY: And he didn't. So okay, was he a lousy lover?

CUCA: Who said anything about lousy?! He didn't please me. Maybe I didn't please him either.

CAMMY: What?

CUCA: Two people promise to love each other forever and one of them always loves more than the other. Gives more.

CAMMY: Wait a second. Raul didn't give?

CUCA: Gave different. Felt he didn't have to prove anything anymore. Maybe "prove" is the wrong word.

CAMMY: You probably put a gun to the poor man's head screaming, "Prove you love me!" Boy, is that attractive. That would do it for me.

CUCA: Okay, it was me, then. That's what you wanted to hear, right? ...I wish he had something in him. I wish I was the cause of it. He'd get angry at politicians. He'd see them on television and holler and curse at them and I always got so angry I'd have to leave the room. All that passion and none of it for me.

CAMMY: Oh, all you wanted was a little-

CUCA: (Cutting her off) I wanted him to want me. You see the way I dress. Tight this, tight that. Men notice me, they look at me. Even when I was with him they looked at me, but he, he still didn't see me.

CAMMY: Maybe you weren't his type anymore.

(CUCA *begins to cry.*)

CAMMY: Hey look, I was just teasing you.

CUCA: No, you're right, I wasn't his type anymore.
I changed. Fat, skinny, blonde, brunette. I could be
everything he wanted except new. I can't be new no
more.

(RAYMOND's *apartment*)

RAYMOND: The subject is closed. I don't want a Spanish
name for the baby. There, I said it, okay? You only
have like six gazillion names to choose from. So drop
the Hector, drop the Jose, I'm not going to have him
grow up to be one of those punks you see on the
subway. I am not going to add a Guillermo to his load.
No. Listen to what I'm saying. I've done everything
you've wanted but this is non negotiable. No Spanish
names.

(*Factory.* CUCA *is on the assembly line.* RAYMOND *enters.*)

CUCA: Ramon.

RAYMOND: (*Quickly correcting her*) Mister Rivers. Uh,
Ms Valdez, I was wondering if you would be interested
in my tutoring you in English.

(CAMMY *enters.*)

CUCA: (*To* CAMMY) What did he say? What did he say?

RAYMOND: You understand English.

CUCA: Not when you talk like that.

(CAMMY *laughs.* RAYMOND *glares at her.*)

CAMMY: I'll translate.

RAYMOND: Don't you have work to do?

CUCA: English classes?

CAMMY: Oooh. Private?

RAYMOND: Don't you want to be better than what you are? Tell her this is a great opportunity.

CAMMY: So sorry. No speaka da English. Excuse me, but what the hell is the matter with the way she is now?

CUCA: What does he want?

CAMMY: Hold on a second.

RAYMOND: If she has a chance to better herself she'd be stupid not to take it.

CUCA: Hello? Hello, please, I'm here.

RAYMOND: Are you going to translate or not?

CAMMY: He thinks you're broken, he thinks he can fix you.

CUCA: What? He didn't say that.

CAMMY: Same difference. Just tell him, "no thank you".

RAYMOND: Me teach.

CAMMY: Oh brother.

CUCA: When?

RAYMOND: Today, right after work.

CUCA: I food shop Friday.

CAMMY: Too bad.

RAYMOND: I don't believe you. I'm begging you so I can do you a favor. It would be good for you.

CUCA: When?

RAYMOND: Tomorrow? Or will you still be in the middle of your shopping frenzy?

CUCA: Okay.

CAMMY: *(Mimicking her)* Okay.

RAYMOND: Where?

(CUCA *shrugs.*)

CAMMY: How about my house?

RAYMOND: We'll meet at the Staten Island Ferry. A very public place. Remember to bring a pencil and some paper.

CUCA: Uh huh.

(CAMMY *and* CUCA *stare at* RAYMOND.)

RAYMOND: Well, have a lovely remainder of the day. *(He awkwardly makes his exit.)*

CAMMY: I don't like him cause he's stuck up. Don't look at nobody, don't talk to nobody.

CUCA: He talks to me.

CAMMY: That's cause he thinks you're easy. …You ain't, right?

(CUCA *playfully hits* CAMMY *and goes back to work.)*

CAMMY: He's a big executive so he think he's better than everybody. Big shot Mister Rivers.

CUCA: *(Almost to herself)* Rivera.

CAMMY: What Rivera?

CUCA: Nothing; you got a big mouth.

CAMMY: Is his name Rivera?

CUCA: I ain't gonna tell you.

CAMMY: And the bastard don't speak Spanish?

CUCA: Mind your own business.

CAMMY: Don't talk to me like that. That's something he would say.

CUCA: I'm sorry.

CAMMY: You see him so big and important and he's afraid of me. He knows I am as ugly as I am honest and I will tell him the truth to his face.

CUCA: Cammy.

CAMMY: Go ahead, take you class. But the only thing he want to teach you is how to forget.

(Saturday. 10:15 A M. RAYMOND is at the Staten Island Ferry. He is wearing the same suit he wore the previous day. He has obviously been drinking and is in the middle of what is probably his second hangover. Nonetheless, he continues drinking. CUCA arrives. She is wearing a house dress and rollers on her head, covered by a colorful bandana. She is in full makeup.)

RAYMOND: You're late.

CUCA: Yeah.

RAYMOND: What is it with you people and time?

CUCA: Sorry.

RAYMOND: Sorry don't mean shit. It's not like I don't have other things to do, you know. Learning English is to your benefit. I mean, what do I get out of this?

(CUCA spots the ferry.)

CUCA: The ferry.

RAYMOND: It's just a stinking subway on the water, that's all.

CUCA: It's pretty.

RAYMOND: No, an ocean liner is pretty. I can see I'm going to have to teach you taste as well. Just kidding.

CUCA: *(With an edge)* Oh yeah.

RAYMOND: …Let's get some coffee.

CUCA: No, no café.

RAYMOND: I meant real coffee.

CUCA: No, teach.

RAYMOND: Right now? Gee, I don't know. Do you think there are enough distractions for you? It's like an oven in here.

(CUCA *sits down and takes a notebook and pencil from her bag. She also checks her make up in her compact and powders her face. She looks at her watch.*)

CUCA: Two hours.

RAYMOND: As if you're doing me a favor.

(CUCA *closes her compact and returns it to her purse which she very purposely snaps shut.* RAYMOND *sits by her.*)

RAYMOND: You wear too much make up.

CUCA: You drink too much.

RAYMOND: *(Laughs)* Well, that's enough English for one day. I kind of miss your thermos, don't you?

CUCA: Oh yeah, the thermos.

RAYMOND: No café.

CUCA: Very good.

(RAYMOND *smiles.*)

RAYMOND: With your permission. *(He takes a swig from his bottle.)* Not the classiest thing I've ever done, but I don't have to impress you, right Cuca?

CUCA: Right. Why drink?

RAYMOND: The buzz. Calms me. You wouldn't know it by looking at me but I'm a very nervous man.

(RAYMOND *pantomimes nervous.* CUCA *laughs.*)

CUCA: Too bad.

RAYMOND: There's this great thin line where it just feels so perfect. Everything falls into place. And I start drinking faster and faster thinking I'll get there sooner and I wind up going right past it. But for a brief second, I'm perfect. I'm right. Hey, you read and write

in Spanish, don't you? Of course you do. You're not
totally illiterate.

CUCA: I don't understand.

RAYMOND: Read, write, Spanish.

CUCA: Yes.

RAYMOND: I kind of got you here under false pretenses.
I need your help. I mean, I'll teach you English if you
want, but actually I need a little of your Spanish today.
(He pulls a birthday greeting card from his jacket pocket.) I
want to send a birthday card to my son in Puerto Rico.

CUCA: Okay.

RAYMOND: Yeah, uh well. He speaks English, you
know. He's a bright boy. But, I uh, wanted to show him
I could send him something in Spanish. Could you do
that for me?

CUCA: What I write?

RAYMOND: Write it on your pad and I'll do it over in
my handwriting.

CUCA: You love him?

RAYMOND: Yeah, but don't write that.

CUCA: Why?

RAYMOND: Look, I'm asking you for a favor. A favor
is something for somebody else. You don't have to
approve of it. You don't want to do it? Fine. I'll get
somebody else.

CUCA: Who?

RAYMOND: I'm sorry. I didn't mean to blow up. ...I
don't know anybody else. Please.

CUCA: *Por favor.*

RAYMOND: *(Smiles)* Yeah, well a little *por favor* to you
too.

(CUCA *begins to write.*)

CUCA: *Querido hijo.*

(RAYMOND *takes a swig.*)

RAYMOND: *Querido hijo,* that's good.

CUCA: *Feliz cumpleaños, en este tu dia.*

RAYMOND: Happy birthday *en este tu dia.*

CUCA: *Es el deseo de tu padre.*

RAYMOND: *Tu padre.*

CUCA: More?

RAYMOND: No, that's plenty. I'll just sign it. Thanks a lot.

CUCA: Welcome.

RAYMOND: You're welcome.

CUCA: You're welcome.

RAYMOND: I want to send my business card. Is that stupid?

CUCA: No.

RAYMOND: I'm the first one in my family to have a job in an office. Nobody ever did before me. I sent one of my cards to my mother. I'm sure they framed it. They're like that.

(RAYMOND *shows* CUCA *his business card.*)

CUCA: Why "Raymond Rivers"?

RAYMOND: That's who I am. I tried to exlplain it to Connie but she would say, "What are you talking about?" So I stopped. I don't want her to think less of me. We've broken up and made up a dozen times. The last time was the worst. Then she found out she was pregnant and told me, "Okay, you get one more chance." ...So I don't drink...in front of her.

CUCA: So don't drink.

RAYMOND: So how about you? Aren't you supposed to be some kind of baby factory.

CUCA: No. *(She points to her stomach.)* Empty. Never.

RAYMOND: First Puerto Rican woman I ever met who didn't have a litter of kids.

CUCA: What's litter?

RAYMOND: You know, like when a cat has kittens.

CUCA: *(An edge)* Ah. I tell you if I have a litter of anything.

RAYMOND: What?

CUCA: Nothing. English class over. You're welcome. *(She gets up and exits.)*

(CUCA's usual cafeteria.)

COOK: (V O) So, ham and eggs, lady?

CUCA: French toast, please. With syrup extra. Excuse me, extra syrup.

(CAMMY addresses the factory workers.)

CAMMY: So ladies, we got ourselves a memo from management. Oh yeah. It says—

CUCA: (Under her breath) Reads.

CAMMY: Irregardless of the weather, halter tops cannot be worn on the work floor.

CUCA: Regardless.

CAMMY: That's what I said.

CUCA: No, you said irregardless.

CAMMY: (Hisses) Don't correct me in front of the girls!

CUCA: I'm just saying—

CAMMY: That you know more than me now? A couple of classes with that pendejo and you're British all of a sudden?

(CUCA *takes the memo from* CAMMY)

CUCA: Where do you see the word "irregardless"?

(*There is a stand off.*)

CAMMY: …*Vete al carajo!* (*She storms off.*)

(RAYMOND *at his desk.*)

RAYMOND: (*On the phone*) Yeah, I was thinking, you know maybe it's best for my parents to just come to the wedding. Their English is sort of non existent and they're just going to feel uncomfortable at the reception. I'm just thinking about what's best for them, you know. Yeah, I know you love them, that's really sweet, honey, but they're just gonna feel out of place. Sitting them with your parents, what are they supposed to say to each other? Look it's better for them if I take them out to a nice dinner the night before the wedding and just take them back to the hotel right after the ceremony. I know them, they'd prefer that. They're good people you know, how did they ever have a punk like me, huh? I'm kidding. They're very proud of me.

(*The Factory.* CAMMY *and* RAYMOND *cross paths.*)

CAMMY: Good morning, Mister Rivera.

(CAMMY *smirks and continues on her way.* RAYMOND *stops her.*)

RAYMOND: First of all, when you address me you do it with respect. Secondly, my name is Rivers. That's the name on my door and that's the name I go by.

CAMMY: Man, all I said was "good morning".

RAYMOND: Hey, I'm talking to you! You call me Mister Rivers. You ever call me anything else and you'll be out of a job. Do you understand me?

CAMMY: *Si señor.*

RAYMOND: *(Walking away)* You're fired.

CAMMY: Hey man, you can't do that.

(RAYMOND keeps walking.)

CAMMY: I'll take it to the union. Maybe I'll take it to your bosses. I'm not going to beg for my job. I swear to God, I'm not gonna beg.

(CUCA goes to RAYMOND's office.)

CUCA: I gotta talk to you.

RAYMOND: How much do you need your job.

CUCA: I need it a lot.

RAYMOND: Then get out.

CUCA: You can't fire Cammy cause my mistake. Look, she not gonna tell nobody. She promise.

RAYMOND: I don't give a shit who she tells. Do you think I'm afraid of her? Who's she going to tell? All her cronies from her minimum wage minimum brain pool? Maybe they'll get a laugh out of it but they're stuck down there for the rest of their lives. I am not like them. I have never been like them. Now, if you'll excuse me, I have work to do and I'm sure you have work to do. So why don't you go back to whatever idiotic task it is you do for a living.

CUCA: You should show people some respect.

RAYMOND: Respect? Hey lady, I trusted you.

CUCA: You respect me!

(RAYMOND dismisses CUCA with his hand.)

RAYMOND: I thought you were better than her kind. I was trying to make somebody out of you.

(CUCA *throws her purse at* RAYMOND.)

CUCA: *(She hits her chest for emphasis)* I am somebody! I deserve respect!

RAYMOND: You better leave now.

(CUCA *retrieves her purse. Some items have fallen out, among them her compact. She opens it, the glass is broken. She sits on the floor and cries.)*

RAYMOND: Hey, come on, don't do that. I'll get you another one.

(RAYMOND *tries to soothe* CUCA, *she shakes him off.)*

RAYMOND: You'll wear a little less make up, so what? It's not all bad.

CUCA: My mother die when I seven. She call me to her and put make up on me. She told me she want to see what her little girl would look like as a woman. I was crying, so make up kept falling, running. She keep saying, "Please, Cuquita, just let mami see." *(She clutches the compact.)* Hers.

RAYMOND: I'm sorry.

CUCA: No, if it were about you, then you sorry. *(She gets up to exit.)*

RAYMOND: Please don't go. Look, Cammy can keep her job.

(CUCA *ignores* RAYMOND.)

RAYMOND: What do you want?

(CUCA *exits.)*

RAYMOND: I expect you back tomorrow, Ms Valdez. Do you hear me?

(CUCA *arrives home. She takes off her coat. A knock is heard, she opens the door to* CAMMY. *They stare at each other.*)

CAMMY: They call me. They gave me my job back. Thanks to your Mister Rivers who got me fired in the first place.

CUCA: He's not mine.

CAMMY: I'm sorry.

CUCA: Well, I quit.

CAMMY: Because of me?

CUCA: Cause of me. You can't force somebody to respect you.

CAMMY: Tell that to Rivera, sorry Rivers. Can I come in?

CUCA: ...I yelled at him.

CAMMY: Good for you.

CUCA: I've been married and divorced three times and this is the first time I ever yelled at a man. I just never could. Now all of a sudden I'm working, I'm yelling at men. Now he'll hate me.

CAMMY: He's not gonna hate you. ...Had you just stayed my friend none of this would have happened.

CUCA: Come in.

(CAMMY *does. Silence.* CUCA *laughs.*)

CUCA: Tonight, I'm horny.

CAMMY: *(Laughs)* I knew you were normal. Wait a second, I got my horny song on the walkman. Listen to this.

(CAMMY *passes her headphones to* CUCA. *After a few beats of the song* CUCA *is nodding enthusiastically.*)

CUCA: I know exactly what she means.

(CUCA *takes the headphones off and pulls* CAMMY *over to the window.*)

CUCA: See the apartment with the yellow curtains?

CAMMY: Uh huh.

CUCA: Every night, like clockwork, the husband and wife do it.

CAMMY: Do it so you can see it?

CUCA: No, do it for themselves. They don't know I'm seeing it.

CAMMY: Get outta here.

CUCA: And he always falls asleep before she can finish. So she has to finish on her own.

CAMMY: Poor thing. What am I saying, "poor thing"? At least she's not faking it with batteries. ...Let's go out.

CUCA: Now?

CAMMY: Sure now. Why not now?

CUCA: I got to look for work tomorrow.

CAMMY: Bullshit. He likes you. You show up tomorrow and he'll be all 'sweetie' and 'honey'. He's a boss, but first he's a man. And I know from men. If anything, act pissed off. That'll get to him. Men like to get yelled at. It grounds them. So get your cha cha heels, girl, cause we're gonna burn tonight!

(RAYMOND *is in the locker room.* CUCA *enters.*)

RAYMOND: Can I see you a second?

(CUCA *shrugs.*)

RAYMOND: Congratulate me. I got a raise yesterday.

CUCA: Congratulate.

RAYMOND: Congratulations. ...You hurt me when you left the way you did yesterday. You didn't give me a

chance to properly apologize. I'm sorry if you think I
don't respect you.

CUCA: You don't.

RAYMOND: Cuquita.

CUCA: Don't call me that.

(RAYMOND *gives* CUCA *a gift.*)

CUCA: What's this?

RAYMOND: It's a present.

(CUCA *opens it. Inside is an expensive and very beautiful
small evening bag.*)

CUCA: Ramon.

RAYMOND: Society ladies carry their compacts in
evening bags. Beautiful, tasteful little bags. Now
you have someplace to carry your compact in. Your
compact is very pretty. Cause it's the real thing, like
you.

CUCA: I can't take this.

RAYMOND: This is part of the apology, Cuca. Don't ruin
it. I give you a gift, I'm sincerely sorry, I smile.

CUCA: No thank you.

(CUCA *gives* RAYMOND *back the gift.*)

RAYMOND: How'd you like to work for me? I mean as
my assistant.

CUCA: I can't type. My English bad.

RAYMOND: We got typists coming out of the ying yang
here. Your English keeps getting better and better.
I want somebody on my side. Someone I can trust.
You're a bright woman, Cuca. You'd work in my office.
You could dress nice to come to work. Forget all about
that prefab cottage in your Puerto Rico. How about it?

CUCA: No, but thank you.

RAYMOND: I can talk to you. I can tell you things I can never tell anybody else. We almost always fight, but we always make up, don't we? Why do you want to go to Puerto Rico? Who am I going to talk to if you leave?

CUCA: You talk to Connie. That's who you're supposed to talk to.

RAYMOND: No. It never comes out right. I look at her when she's asleep and I wonder when this drug called love is going to wear off. Is she going to wake up one day and say, "Wait a second, you're not who I thought you were." ...Look, I'll see you a little later. Glad you're back. Dinner?

CUCA: ...Okay.

RAYMOND: Good. Thanks. *(He exits.)*

(The Executive Dining Room. CUCA *puts a little tape player on the table. Salsa plays.* RAYMOND *enters.)*

RAYMOND: Oh God. Jungle music.

*(*CUCA *laughs. She picks up the tape player.)*

CUCA: I just bought it. *(She begins to dance.)* You can't dance?

RAYMOND: Not to that. I admit it.

*(*CUCA *laughs and stretches her arms to* RAYMOND.*)*

CUCA: Come on.

RAYMOND: Yeah, right.

CUCA: I teach. You surprise Connie.

RAYMOND: Forget it.

CUCA: You teach me English. I teach you salsa.

RAYMOND: Cuca, we are at work.

*(*CUCA *sits down.)*

RAYMOND: Could you please lower the volume?

(Silence except for the small sound of salsa in the background)

RAYMOND: Everybody's gone, but we are still at work. We are professionals.

CUCA: Yes, sir.

RAYMOND: I saw Mister Stark in the hall earlier. He said he was very impressed with the work coming out of my department. I looked him straight and the eye and said, "You should be".

(CUCA whoops, jumps up and raises the volume on the tape player.)

RAYMOND: Sssh. Not that loud.

CUCA: Everybody gone.

(RAYMOND is silent for a moment.)

RAYMOND: Okay, just let me have a shot of café.

(CUCA gives RAYMOND his cup and he gulps his spiked coffee.)

CUCA: Here we go.

RAYMOND: Yeah, just don't go nuts on me.

(CUCA and RAYMOND stand facing each other. She tries to move slower to accommodate him. He is totally inept.)

CUCA: *(Puts her hands on his hips)* Come on. Move this.

RAYMOND: I think I should just stick to café.

CUCA: We do slow.

RAYMOND: This is your idea of slow? How can you dance in those things? My mother used to wear heels like that.

CUCA: Oh yeah?

RAYMOND: Every Saturday night. *(His movements become looser.)*

CUCA: Botate!

(RAYMOND *reaches for his jacket pocket and drinks his liquor straight. He makes a face and shudders. She takes the bottle and puts it on the table behind her. She smiles and shakes her head "no".*)

RAYMOND: Okay, let's try this stuff again.

(CUCA *laughs as they dance. He is almost her equal. The music heats up and she cuts loose.*)

RAYMOND: Hey, wait, wait, wait!

(CUCA *continues her frenetic pace.*)

CUCA: Come on. Come on.

(RAYMOND *shakes his head, laughs and tries.*)

CUCA: Gimme hand.

(RAYMOND *does.* CUCA *is an expert and makes him look far better than he is. Lights begin to fade. He lets out a loud laugh.*)

(CUCA*'s apartment. The phone rings.*)

CUCA: Hello?

RAYMOND: Cuca, this is Ray. Uh, Connie just gave birth. Just now.

CUCA: Congratulations.

RAYMOND: Thanks, thanks. It's a boy. So, we're going to get married in a month or so. Once Connie goes down a couple of dress sizes. She'd kill me if she heard me say that. I really love her Cuca.

CUCA: That's good. That's how it should be.

RAYMOND: I want you to meet Connie, and like, get to know her. And you know, when you start seeing somebody maybe we can all go out to dinner. There are a lot of guys at the company who just have to get to know you a little better to see how special you really are. I'm going to marry you into management.

CUCA: And what if that's not what I want?

RAYMOND: Then you're crazy.

CUCA: It's what you want. It's not what I want.

RAYMOND: Would you like to be the baby's godmother?

CUCA: It's okay with Connie?

RAYMOND: No problem.

CUCA: Baby visit me in Aibonito?

RAYMOND: I don't think so.

CUCA: You and Connie come to visit me?

RAYMOND: No.

(CAMMY *and* RAYMOND *in the corridor.*)

CAMMY: Excuse mister, Mister Rivers. Cuca is leaving for Puerto Rico at the end of the week and we are doing a small collection for her. Would you like to donate?

RAYMOND: Did you ask anybody else from management?

CAMMY: No. But I thought you were friends.

RAYMOND: So this is a collection just the shop girls are doing?

CAMMY: The shop women.

(*Pause.* RAYMOND *takes out his wallet and gives her all his money.*)

RAYMOND: If she asks, this is from everybody.

CAMMY: Thank you.

(RAYMOND *nods and walks away.*)

(The locker room. RAYMOND *is sitting on a bench. Enter* CUCA.)

RAYMOND: Last day, huh?

CUCA: Yeah.

RAYMOND: That used to be my locker over there. I think it still has some of my graffiti on the inside. You look very beautiful tonight.

CUCA: I look like I always look.

RAYMOND: No, tonight you look…

CUCA: Have you been drinking?

RAYMOND: Haven't you heard? I don't drink anymore.

CUCA: Promise?

RAYMOND: Promise.

CUCA: Fool. You were happy before you met me and you'll be happy after I go. That's good. That's how it should be.

RAYMOND: I have no right to say anything to you.

CUCA: You're my friend. You got rights.

RAYMOND: Your friend wants you to stay.

CUCA: Don't you want me to be happy?

RAYMOND: Nah.

*(*CUCA *and* RAYMOND *both laugh.)*

RAYMOND: Who am I going to have café with? Who am I going to teach English to?

CUCA: Who am I going to teach salsa to?

RAYMOND: Who's going to be my Puerto Rico?

CUCA: I know you didn't chose me as a friend. I barge in and forced my friendship on you. I know that.

RAYMOND: Hey Cuquita, I hate you.

CUCA: Same to you.

(RAYMOND *doesn't answer. Pause.* CUCA *takes her coat.*)

CUCA: Bye bye.

RAYMOND: A friend who loves me as I am. Who I have sometimes been so cruel to and still loves me. I don't think God is going to give me this again.

CUCA: Ramon.

RAYMOND: Cause I don't deserve it.

CUCA: ...One last favor. I give you Spanish lesson. Translate, please. *Yo te amo.*

RAYMOND: I...

CUCA: Please.

RAYMOND: I love you.

CUCA: *Porque eres un hombre bueno.*

RAYMOND: Because you are, I am a good man.

CUCA: *Y si he llorado por ti.*

RAYMOND: And if I have cried over you.

CUCA: *Ha sido mi desicion.*

RAYMOND: It has been my decision.

CUCA: *Eres testaduro.*

RAYMOND: What?

CUCA: Stubborn.

RAYMOND: *Testaduro.*

CUCA: Dominating.

RAYMOND: *Dominante.*

CUCA: Bad tempered.

RAYMOND: *Mal humerado.*

CUCA: And my friend.

RAYMOND: *Y mi amigo.* What will I do without you?

CUCA: Hey, this is my class. ...*Te quiero Ramon Rivera.*

RAYMOND: I love you Raymond...

(CUCA *puts her fingers on* RAYMOND'*s lip, silencing him.*)

CUCA: *Por favor. (She removes her fingers.)*

RAYMOND: I love you...Ramon Rivera.

CUCA: Very good. ...Very, very good.

(CUCA *gets up and exits. Slow fade to:)*

(Blackout)

END OF PLAY

www.ingramcontent.com/pod-product-compliance
Lightning Source LLC
Chambersburg PA
CBHW070033110426
42741CB00035B/2757